Best Stories for Six Year Olds

Also available from Hodder Story Collections

- Best Stories for Under Fives
- Best Stories for Five Year Olds
- Best Stories for Seven Year Olds

BEST STORIES FOR SIX YEAR OLDS

BY HELEN CRESSWELL

LEON ROSSELSON

MARY RAYNER

DAVID HENRY WILSON

AND SHARON CREECH

Illustrated by Anthony Lewis

Spelling Lesson © Helen Cresswell 1995
Uproar in Yukland © Leon Rosselson 1995
Rupert the Second © Mary Rayner 1995
The Stinky Tree © David Henry Wilson 1995
My Brother is a Pig © Sharon Creech 1995

This collection © Hodder Children's Books 1995
Illustrations © Anthony Lewis 1995

First published in Great Britain in 1995 by
Hodder Children's Books

The right of the authors to be identified as the Authors of the
Work has been asserted by them in accordance with the
Copyright, Designs and Patents Act 1988.

10 9 8 7 6 5 4 3 2 1

All rights reserved. No part of this publication may be
reproduced, stored in a retrieval system, or transmitted, in any
form or by any means without the prior written permission of
the publisher, nor be otherwise circulated in any form of binding
or cover other than that in which it is published and without a
similar condition being imposed on the subsequent purchaser.

All characters in this publication are fictitious and any
resemblance to real persons, living or dead, is purely
coincidental.

A Catalogue record for this book is available from the British
Library

ISBN 0340 646349

Typeset by
Avon Dataset Ltd, Bidford on Avon, Warwickshire B50 4JH

Printed and bound in Great Britain by
Cox & Wyman Ltd, Reading, Berks.

Hodder Children's Books
A Division of Hodder Headline plc
338 Euston Road
London NW1 3BH

Contents

Spelling Lesson
by Helen Cresswell 1

Uproar in Yukland
by Leon Rosselson 21

Rupert the Second
by Mary Rayner 37

The Stinky Tree
by David Henry Wilson 53

My Brother is a Pig
by Sharon Creech 65

Spelling Lesson

Helen Cresswell

Spelling Lesson

Helen Cresswell

Victoria Lucy Emmett was six years eight months and two days old when it happened. (Most people can't remember when they learned to spell, but she can.) She lived at number six Meadow Lane with her father and mother and brother Ben. He was eight years and goodness knows how many months and days. He called his sister Sicky Vicky when he felt like it, and she called him Clever Clogs.

Victoria believed in magic. She believed in witches, genies in bottles, gingerbread houses and giants. Ben didn't.

"You'd better watch out!" she told him. "Don't you even believe in *wishes*?"

"They don't work," he told her. "Last birthday I wished for a new bike till I nearly *bust*, and I still didn't get one. Wishes are rubbish."

"What about spells? Don't you even believe in spells?"

"No such thing," he said. "Why don't you grow up, Sicky Vicky?"

"Oh *you*, Clever Clogs! You'd better watch out!"

And off she went to make a spell. She didn't really know where to start, having never made a spell before.

"You need a recipe," she thought, "and you need special words. Recipe first. Pity a witch doesn't live next door."

Who actually lived next door was Miss Drake, who was amazingly old and had a black cat called Graymalkin. She grew herbs in her tiny garden and dried them in her kitchen. She was definitely the next best thing to a witch.

Spelling Lesson

Victoria went round and knocked on her door. Miss Drake opened it. She was wearing black, as usual.

"Good morning, Miss Drake," said Victoria politely.

"It might be," replied Miss Drake. "We shall have to see."

"I just wondered if you had some herbs to spare," said Victoria. "I want to make a spell."

"A ssspell..." repeated Miss Drake, in a hissing kind of way. She smiled, and her face cracked into a thousand wrinkles. Her eyes, which were green, glittered. "There's a pretty thought, my dear. You had better come in."

So for the first time Victoria went into the poky little house, down a dark passage and into the kitchen. Bunches of herbs hung from hooks. Graymalkin lay by the fire growling, and above the fire was a large black cauldron. It bubbled and simmered and steamed and certainly did not smell like anyone's dinner.

"A ssspell..." said Miss Drake again. "What kind of a spell? Go invisible... fly through the air... turn toad?"

"*That's* an idea!" said Victoria, who hadn't

really thought what the spell would be. "Turn toad!"

"Who?" enquired Miss Drake. "You?"

"Oh no!" said Victoria hastily. "Ben! You know – the one who's always kicking balls into your garden. *And* he doesn't believe in magic."

"Ah!" said Miss Drake. "Him!"

"Thinks he knows everything," Victoria told her. "Clever Clogs. Serve him right to be turned toad. Have you got some good things to mix up?"

Miss Drake had. The pair prepared the mixture together. Victoria ground the herbs with a pestle and mortar, while Miss Drake carefully ladled the liquid from the cauldron and measured dark tinctures from a row of bottles on the shelves.

"What does your brother like to drink?" she asked.

"Well, he quite likes coffee, but Mum doesn't let him have it very often," said Victoria. "She says it's bad for him. *She* drinks it though, lots of it."

Miss Drake let Victoria tip her herbs into the mixture, then heated it in a saucepan. It

Spelling Lesson

looked – and funnily enough smelled – exactly like coffee.

"Shouldn't there be a frog's leg?" asked Victoria. "Or hair of cat? And what about the words?"

"Oh, that's the easy part," Miss Drake told her, and began to mumble and mutter as she stirred. Victoria couldn't catch the words, but they sounded quite spellish.

"There!" Miss Drake poured the steaming mixture into a blue mug. "Quickly, now, before it gets cold!"

Victoria picked up the mug and carried it carefully through to the passage and Miss Drake opened the front door to let her out. Back home, Victoria could see her mother in the garden, weeding. On the kitchen table stood a steaming mug of coffee.

"Better find Ben quickly, before Mum sees," she thought. She put her own mug down and went to fetch him. He was making a kite from a kit.

"Toads don't fly kites," Victoria thought, "so *I* shall be able to have it."

"*What?*" he said when she told him. "Coffee? You're barmy. Any case, you're not allowed

Spelling Lesson

to muck around with the stove. *Or* the kettle."

She hadn't thought of that. She began to wish she had chosen orange juice instead of coffee. On the other hand, surely even clever Miss Drake could not have made *that* concoction look and taste like orange juice.

"Well anyway, I did," she said. "Come *on*."

"No fear!" said Ben. "It's a trick."

"It is not!"

" 'Tis."

" 'T'isn't."

" 'Tis."

" 'T'isn't."

Victoria felt quite desperate. It looked as though a perfectly good spell was going to waste.

"I bet you it isn't!" she said.

He looked at her.

"Bet me what?"

"Bet you . . . bet you . . ." she couldn't for the life of her think what.

"Your pocket money?" he suggested.

She did not hesitate. It would easily be worth fifty pence to see Ben turned toad.

"All right," she said. "Come *on*!"

He got up and followed her downstairs. Her

heart went hammer hammer hammer. Now it was going to happen. Clever Clogs would turn toad under her very eyes.

"There!" She pushed open the kitchen door and pointed triumphantly at the mug of steaming coffee. Ben boggled.

"You'll catch it if mum finds out!" was all he said.

"Go on then – drink it!"

"Still think it's fishy. Bet you've put salt in it."

"No I have not! Taste it!"

He picked up the coffee. Her heart went hammer hammer hammer. He sipped it. He sipped again. Victoria held her breath.

"Not bad," he said grudgingly.

He was still Ben, not a toad. Perhaps he had to drink all of it?

He fetched the biscuit tin and sat down. Victoria watched him.

She did not take her eyes off him for a single instant. She did not want to miss the actual, magical moment when he would turn toad.

"Where's Mum?" he asked, dunking a biscuit.

"In the garden."

Spelling Lesson

"Dunno what she'll say, if she—"

He stopped. He stared. His eyes bulged.

"This is it!" she thought. "He's turning!"

Toads have bulging eyes.

He went on boggling. His mug went down plonk on the table, his mouth opened and closed but no sound came out.

"Perhaps he can only croak now," Victoria thought. "But why's he not shrinking? And why's he not going all brown and leathery?"

He pointed. She turned. She boggled. Her mouth opened and closed but no sound came out.

There, squatting by the sink, was a huge toad. It was brown and khaki with eyes like marbles. Its mouth opened and closed but no sound came out.

"Oh help!" said Victoria faintly.

Ben pushed back his chair and ran to the back door.

"Mum!" he yelled. "Quick!" Silence. Then, "She's not there. Thought you said she was in the garden."

Victoria's eyes travelled up from the squatting toad to the draining board. There, empty, was a blue mug.

Stories for Six Year Olds

She looked at the toad.

"Oh Mum!" she whispered. "What've I done?"

The toad looked mournfully back at her.

"Dirty great thing!" said Ben. "How did it get in here?"

"It's Mum!" said Victoria. Her voice came out all squeaky.

"You *what*?"

"It's Mum. Oh Mum, I didn't mean it!"

Ben seized the sweeping brush propped by the door.

"Look out!"

"No!" screamed Victoria. "Don't! You'll hurt her!"

She grabbed hold of the handle and tried to pull it away. This way and that they tugged while the toad sat watching with glassy eyes.

"It's Mum, it really is, it's Mum!"

"Idiot – give it *here*!"

"I did a spell – it was meant for you! *You* should be a toad!"

Ben let go of the brush.

"Go on then," he said. "Spit it out."

So she told him. She told him about her visit

Spelling Lesson

to Miss Drake, and how the two of them had mixed the spell together.

"And I meant it to be *you*!" she wailed.

"Thank you very much," he said.

"And now we've got a toad for a mother! What'll we do, what'll we do?"

"You're making the whole thing up," Ben said. "Must be. No such thing as spells."

"That's what you always say!"

"Mum's about somewhere. She wouldn't just go out and leave us. Mum! Mum!"

In the silence that followed the toad made a little series of jumps forward – hop hop hop!

"Oh help!" Ben said. "It heard me!" He backed away.

"*Now* do you believe me? I don't like it, I don't like it!"

And Victoria began to cry. Her own dear mother was now a hideous toad and it was all her fault.

"Cry baby," Ben said. "It's no use blubbing. Dad'll kill you when he gets home. Are you *sure* it's her? No such thing as spells."

This time, he didn't sound quite so certain.

"If there *were* such things as spells," he went on, "I suppose there must be a way of *un*spelling them."

Victoria stopped crying. She stared, first at the toad with its pulsing double chin, then at Ben.

"*I* don't know how," she said, "but perhaps Miss Drake does."

"Well you'd better get round there fast and ask her," he told her.

Victoria hesitated. Miss Drake had been all very well when she *was* Miss Drake. Now it looked as if she were a real live witch.

"You'll have to come with me," she said.

Spelling Lesson

"I'll stop and keep an eye on *that*. If it hops off, we're sunk."

"We can shut the doors to keep it in. I'm not going by myself."

"Oh, all *right*!" He banged shut the door that led to the hall.

"You stop there, ugly mug!" he told the toad.

They both went out of the back door and shut it behind them. Next door, Victoria took a deep breath and knocked.

The door opened. Miss Drake looked from one to the other.

"I'm sorry to trouble you Miss Drake this is Ben!" said Victoria, all in one breath.

"Hmph!" said Miss Drake, and her green eyes narrowed. "Not a toad, then. Why?"

"I – I – it all went wrong," Victoria stammered.

Miss Drake held the door wide.

"You'd better come in."

Back in the tiny kitchen, with Graymalkin still growling and the cauldron still bubbling, Victoria told her story.

"It was a lovely spell, it really was, and it worked," she finished, "but it got the wrong person."

"*You* got the wrong person," Miss Drake corrected. She fixed Ben with her greeny yellowy eyes. "*You* should be a toad!"

He did not reply.

"Don't believe in spells, eh?"

Still he did not reply. He did not even shake his head.

"No he doesn't!" Victoria said. "*Or* witches, *or* wishes, *or* giants! He doesn't believe in *anything*!"

Now there was a very long silence, but for the growling cat and the bubbling cauldron.

"Don't believe must be *made* to believe!" The words were a fierce hiss.

"Oh, don't turn him toad as well!" Victoria wailed. A toad for mother *and* brother would be too much to bear.

"I just wondered . . I just wondered . . . oh, can't you turn her back?"

"*I* can't," said Miss Drake. "But perhaps you can. Or perhaps . . . you!"

She looked at Ben, and grinned. Her face splintered like glass.

"Yessss . . . yesss . . . you!"

"Shall we make another spell?" asked Victoria. The first one might have gone wrong,

Spelling Lesson

but she had enjoyed making it just the same.

"Oh no ... oh no ... that's not the way ..."

"W-what, then?"

Miss Drake shook her head and the grey wisps flew.

"Don't you know your fairy tales? Think, child, think!"

Victoria thought as hard as she knew how, she thought till her brain ached.

"The Frog Prince!" Miss Drake hissed.

Then Victoria remembered. The story of the princess who threw her golden ball into the well, and a frog fetched it out and went to live with her at the palace. That frog ate with her and slept with her and in the end—

"Oh!" she gasped. "Oh no!"

The princess at last had had to *kiss* that frog before he could change back into a handsome prince. Victoria did not think she could kiss that toad. In fact, she *knew* she couldn't.

"I can't!" she wailed. "Oh – I can't!"

"Not you," said Miss Drake calmly. "*Him!*"

Ben looked from one to the other of them. He had not the foggiest idea what they were talking about. He played computer games instead of reading fairy tales.

"He shall do it!" said Miss Drake. "Perhaps then we shall see who doesn't believe in spells! Tell him, child!"

Victoria gulped. An hour ago she had wanted him turned toad. Now she was actually feeling sorry for him. He would have to go down on his hands and knees and put his face forward right up against that pimply brown skin and those bulging eyes and—

"Ugh!" she shuddered at the very thought.

"Tell him," repeated Miss Drake.

So Victoria did, in a trembly voice. Still Ben did not say anything. He had not said a single word since they had come into Miss Drake's house and he had begun to suspect, for the first time in his life, that there might be such things as spells – and witches. He did go pale, though. He went very white indeed.

"*Kisss* it!" said Miss Drake hissingly. "Kissss it! It's the only way."

"It is, Ben, it's true. It might not be too bad. You can just shut your eyes and just – ever so quickly – and it is Mum, remember!"

Ben turned. He marched out of the kitchen and down the passage and Victoria hurried

Spelling Lesson

after him. As they went into the street Miss Drake's triumphant voice followed them:

"Don't believe must be made to believe! Kisss kisss kisss!"

And that is exactly what Ben did. Back in the kitchen, the toad still squatted exactly where they had left it. Ben got down on his hands and knees. He drew an enormous breath and shut his eyes and—

Kiss – whoosh!

It happened so fast that Victoria almost missed it by blinking.

"Oh *do* get from under my feet, Ben!" said Mrs Emmett. "Have you lost something?"

He had – almost. His own mother.

"Funny . . ." she was looking at the table now, and the mug of coffee, no longer steaming. "I could've sworn I'd drunk that . . ."

"She doesn't remember!" thought Victoria. "Oh, thank goodness!"

Then she noticed the empty blue mug on the draining board. Quick as a flash she picked it up and put it behind her back.

"I want you to go to the shop for me, Ben," her mother was saying.

"I'll go with him!" Victoria said.

They would have to take the blue mug back to Miss Drake. She would have to knock, for the third time that morning, on a witch's door.

"And after that," she thought, "I don't think I'll go there again."

Victoria Lucy Emmett had had her first and last spelling lesson. Witches and spells were all very well, she decided, but on the whole they were better kept in story books, where they belong.

Uproar in Yukland

Leon Rosselson

Uproar in Yukland

Leon Rosselson

Underneath the floorboards live the Yuks. Creaky creatures they are with goggle eyes and teeth like macaroni sticks. You may see them as you tiptoe to the fridge on a sleepless summer's night in search of a midnight snack of raspberry jelly and chocolate chip ice cream. And if you do catch sight of them popping up through the cracks in the floorboards, you may wonder how it is possible to tell one Yuk from another Yuk. Because all Yuks look the same. They dress the same. They smell the same. They *are* the same.

Except, of course, for Anton Yuk.

Every morning, at the first croak of the froghorn, the Yuks leap as one out of their mudbags, wash themselves thoroughly in tubs of glue and breakfast on squashed fly sandwiches and mugs of slime tea which they stir with the ends of their noses.

But not Anton Yuk. He lies lazily in a smelly bubbly bath, munching a mouthful of apple pips.

After breakfast, all the Yuks stand to attention and sing the Yuk anthem. This consists of repeating the word YUK in tuneless unison over and over again until they all fall to the ground in a kind of trance.

But not Anton Yuk. He prefers to whistle a trilling tune that he has made up himself.

This does not please the other Yuks. "Anton is bad," they cry. "Anton is disobedient. Be careful, Anton, or you will be punished."

Worst of all, Anton refuses to respect the Yuk greeting. When one Yuk meets another Yuk in the dusty alleyways beneath the floorboards, the polite and proper thing for them to do is to bang their heads together hard and often until both of them crash to the floor unconscious. Don't ask me why they do that. That is what they do and that is what they have always done since the beginning of time and no Yuk has ever thought to question it.

Until Anton Yuk. Anton Yuk, by way of greeting, holds out a hand to be shaken and murmurs "How do you do?"

The other Yuks are shocked. "This is an insult to our sacred customs," they say.

Stories for Six Year Olds

"Besides, shaking hands and saying 'How do you do?' is daft."

"It may be daft," retorts Anton, "but at least it's different. And," he adds, "it doesn't give you a headache."

And so one doomful day, Anton Yuk was brought before the Yuk Elders (or Yackety Yuks, as they were called) and accused of trying to be different. The Yackety Yuks sat on piles of bones in Horatio Yuk Hall which was named after the great Yuk hero who had invented glue. A giant statue of Horatio Yuk bathing in a tub of glue stood in the square outside.

"Your disobedience must be punished," the Yackety Yuks decided. "You will be bound in iron chains and locked deep down in a dark and dismal dungeon until you grovel for forgiveness."

"That'll be the day," said Anton Yuk.

The Yuk Elders, according to their ancient custom, squeezed their noses between their thumbs and forefingers and pronounced (nasally): "We have spoken."

So they took Anton away and bound him in iron chains and locked him deep down in a dark and dismal dungeon. And every morning, the guard brought him his breakfast of slime tea and squashed fly sandwiches. And every evening, another guard (or could it have been the same guard because it's impossible to tell one Yuk from another Yuk) brought him his supper of spider soup and burnt maggot pie.

And every so often, the Yuk Elders sent a messenger to ask if he was ready to grovel for forgiveness.

"That'll be the day," Anton would reply.

So a week passed, or it could have been a month or even a year because being locked deep down in a dark and dismal dungeon made Anton lose all sense of time. It also made him very hungry. He hated slime tea and squashed fly sandwiches and spider soup and especially burnt maggot pie. He left most of it for the guard to gollop down greedily.

What's more he was bored with being bound in iron chains. He wanted to bathe in a smelly bubbly bath. He wanted to munch a mouthful of apple pips. He wanted to be free. But he didn't want to grovel for forgiveness. What was he to do?

"Yukky!" belched the guard one morning

after he'd polished off Anton's breakfast. "Squashed fly sandwiches are my favourite."

"Can I have some apple pips?" asked Anton.

"Forbidden," said the guard.

"Just a mouthful," pleaded Anton.

The goggle-eyed guard glared.

"I'll tell you a joke," Anton said.

"What's a joke?" asked the guard.

"I say something funny and you laugh," explained Anton.

The guard's goggle eyes nearly popped out of his head. "Yuks don't laugh," he said.

It was true. No Yuks had ever been known to laugh. Except Anton Yuk, of course. But doing things that no Yuk had ever been known to do was what had got him into this mess in the first place.

"It'll make you feel delumptious," Anton said, "laughing will."

"What's delumptious?" asked the guard.

"You'll see," said Anton.

"All right," said the guard because he, too, was bored and he thought feeling delumptious might make a change.

So the guard gave Anton a mouthful of apple pips and Anton told the guard this joke.

Uproar in Yukland

"Two Yuks were walking along the alleyways underneath the floorboards. One Yuk fell down a yukhole. The first Yuk shouted down to the Yuk who'd fallen, 'Is it dark down there?' The second Yuk called back, 'I don't know. I can't see a thing.'"

The guard thought about this joke for a minute. Then he said, "I don't feel very delumptious."

"You haven't laughed yet," explained Anton.

"How do you laugh?" asked the guard.

"Ha, ha," said Anton.

"Ha, ha," said the guard.

"Ha, ha, ha," said Anton.

"Ha, ha, ha," repeated the guard.

"Ha, ha, ha, ha, ha, ha," said Anton.

"Ha, ha, ha, ha, ha, ha," echoed the guard.

"Don't stop," said Anton.

"Ha, ha, ha . . ."

Gradually the laughter took hold of the guard, took hold of him body and bone and then heart and soul. He showed his macaroni teeth. He wibbled and wobbled like raspberry jelly. He rolled around the floor. In short, he laughed fit to bust.

"How do you feel?" asked Anton when the

guard had recovered himself.

"Delumptious," said the guard.

"Told you," said Anton. "Want one of my apple pips?"

The next day, another guard brought Anton his breakfast and Anton made the same bargain with him. Apple pips for a joke. That's how it began. Soon all the guards, not wanting to be left out, were asking Anton to tell them jokes so they, too, could feel delumptious. Laughter was spreading through the Yuk nation.

The Yuk Elders were puzzled. Not only were many Yuks going about with mad grins on their faces and showing their macaroni-stick teeth but Anton was still refusing to grovel for forgiveness.

"That'll be the day," was all he would say.

Another week passed (or it could have been a month or even a year). The guard (whichever it was and it doesn't really matter because all Yuks look the same) brought Anton his breakfast and offered him apple pips in exchange for a joke.

"Thank you," said Anton, "but I know a way to make you feel doubly delumptious."

Uproar in Yukland

"What's that feel like?" asked the guard.

"You'll see," said Anton. "First unbind my arms and legs from these iron chains."

"Forbidden," said the guard.

"You'll feel doubly delumptious," promised Anton.

"Oh all right," said the guard. So he did.

Once unbound, Anton held out his hand to be shaken and murmured "How do you do?"

The guard frowned. "That's daft," he said.

"You'll feel doubly delumptious," said Anton.

The guard hesitated. Then, feeling silly, he shook Anton's hand and said: "How do you do?"

"How do you feel?" asked Anton.

"Silly," said the guard.

"Keep practising," said Anton. "You'll get used to it. And then you'll feel—"

"I know," said the guard. "Doubly delumptious."

So the guard kept practising. At first he felt awkward holding out his hand to be shaken and murmuring "How do you do?" when all the other Yuks were banging their heads together. But he soon got used to it. What's more, the bumps on his head disappeared and the pains in his head vanished. In fact, he felt doubly delumptious.

Soon other Yuks began to adopt this new form of greeting just as they had the jokes and the laughter. Arguments arose between these newfanglers, as they were called, and the mudstickers who wanted to follow the old ways.

The Yuk Elders were worried. Not only was Anton Yuk not grovelling for forgiveness but disobedience was breaking out everywhere.

More and more Yuks joined the followers of Anton. They waited eagerly for his next new idea. They began bathing in smelly bubbly baths instead of tubs of glue. It made them feel, they said, doubly doubly delumptious. Then while the mudstickers were singing the old Yuk anthem, the newfanglers started whistling the trilling tune that Anton Yuk had made up himself. What a cacophony!

The Yuk nation was in an uproar. No-one knew what was right or wrong any more. Something had to be done.

And it was. The Yackety Yuks, the Yuk Elders, held an emergency meeting in Horatio

Yuk Hall. The Yuks gathered in the square outside and waited with bated breath. Some of them held their breath for so long they collapsed and had to be carted off to hospital to be revived.

At the day's end, the Yuk Elders sent out a messenger to announce their judgement. This is what they decided. Firstly, all Yuks were now to greet each other by holding out their hands to be shaken and murmuring "How do you do?" instead of all that headbanging. Secondly, all Yuks were to wash in smelly bubbly baths instead of tubs of glue. Thirdly, apple pips were to be munched for breakfast. Fourthly, the old Yuk anthem would no longer be sung. Instead, Anton Yuk's tune would be whistled. Fifthly and lastly, since Anton Yuk was now doing exactly what every other Yuk would be doing, he could no longer be accused of trying to be different. He was to be released at once.

And so order was restored in Yukland. Anton Yuk was released from the dark and dismal dungeon to ear-splitting cries of "Hip hip hooyuki!" The Yuk Elders held out their hands and murmured "How do you do?" And in time, Anton Yuk himself was chosen to be a Yackety Yuk.

And that's why if you do happen to see any Yuks as you tiptoe to the fridge on a sleepless summer's night in search of a midnight snack of raspberry jelly and chocolate chip ice cream, if you do chance to catch sight of any Yuks popping up through the cracks in the floorboards, you will not be able to tell one Yuk from another Yuk. Because all Yuks look the same. They dress the same. They smell the same. They *are* the same.

Except, of course, for Winifred Yuk.

But that's another story.

Rupert the Second

Mary Rayner

Rupert the Second

Mary Rayner

Before Andrew went skating, he went upstairs to check that the snake was still asleep in its box on the window sill.

It was a grass snake. Andrew was looking after it through the school holidays. Not a difficult job, since the snake had gone into its winter sleep some time ago. All that Andrew had to do was keep it cool, and make sure it was all right now and then.

Mr Carpenter, Andrew's teacher, had been going away over Christmas. The snake could not be left in the classroom through the holidays, Mr Carpenter had said. You never knew what the cleaners might do to it, they might mistake it for an adder.

Andrew now knew the difference between an adder and a grass snake. They had different markings, and a grass snake was not poisonous.

Andrew lifted the lid of the box. The snake was coiled round in exactly the same position as the last time he had looked.

"Hello, snake," said Andrew. It needed a name. On the bed was Andrew's battered old teddy, Rupert. That would be a good name for a snake. But perhaps a bit unfair on the teddy? All right then, Rupert the Second.

"Andrew, we're waiting," his sister Liz called up the stairs. Andrew put half a biscuit in the box, just in case Rupert the Second should wake up feeling hungry while he was out skating, shut the lid and thundered downstairs.

"About time," said Elaine, his oldest sister.

Tomorrow was Christmas Day. It was

Mum's idea that they should walk round to the skating rink. "Elaine can help you two with your boots," she'd said. "I don't want you all under foot. There's the turkey to stuff and everything to get ready for James and Kathleen and all their lot coming to Christmas dinner. And there won't be time tomorrow morning, because of opening the presents and then church. Oh and I nearly forgot. The new vicar's having a blessing ceremony at the Family Service, and he wants all of you children to bring your favourite toys and animals. Teddies and things."

I'll take Rupert, thought Andrew as he broke into a run to keep up with Elaine.

Next morning there were some wonderful presents. A brand new football for Andrew, and a Manchester United outfit, and many more. Andrew tried on the outfit at once. It fitted, and looked great. He wanted to have a go with the football, but in no time at all Dad was telling them to get ready for church, and Mum was asking if everybody'd got their things.

Andrew scrambled out of his football gear

and back into his ordinary clothes. He tore upstairs to fetch Rupert.

He was fairly sure that Mum and Dad would say no if he asked, so he opened the box and lifted the snake out carefully. If he undid the zip of his anorak pocket, he could fit him in quite snugly, no one would know. And by the time they reached church it would be all right, because God would know he was a grass snake and not harmful, God knew everything.

In the back of the car Andrew sat up very straight between Liz and Elaine so as not to squash Rupert. They all walked up the centre aisle of the church and sat down in a pew.

Over in one corner was the crib, with a spotlight shining down on it, and candles behind, and wooden figures of Mary and Joseph and the Baby Jesus, the shepherds and the kings, with real straw on the floor. There were more candles fixed to each pillar the whole length of the church, a lot of holly and ivy, and some white flowers up at the top end.

There were a great many people. Andrew had never seen the church so full. It was hot, but he did not dare take off his anorak. He could feel himself going red in the face, but he hoped no one would notice.

They sang several carols, including *The First Noel*. Andrew thought happily about his football, and really let rip on the *Noels*, until Liz dug him in the ribs and hissed "Don't shout."

At last it was time to go up to the altar rail with the other children. Elaine had her china cat, and Liz her fashion doll, and all the others were carrying their toys.

"What about yours?" whispered Mum. "Did you forget?"

Andrew patted his pocket. "No, I've got Rupert here."

"Good boy." Mum smiled down at him.

Elaine and Liz edged out along the pew and led the way up the centre aisle. Andrew followed. They went up the steps and knelt down at the altar rail with all the other children. Behind them, in the body of the church, a baby started to cry, its voice echoing up to the rafters.

The vicar moved along. He was holding out his hands in blessing and smiling what Andrew thought was a soppy smile. He was putting his hands on Elaine's head, and then looking fondly down at her china cat while his lips moved.

The baby's wails changed to a steady yelling. The vicar blessed Liz and her doll, then he moved sideways to face Andrew.

Andrew opened the zip, lifted out Rupert with one hand, and held him up. He uncoiled and hung down. Suddenly he seemed awfully big. So long, now that Andrew was kneeling, that he almost touched the floor.

The baby stopped. There was complete silence in the church. The vicar gave a loud gasp and took several steps backward. In the next instant the baby began again, and Liz screamed.

Andrew scowled at her. Trust her not to know a grass snake when she saw one. But there was no time to say anything to her, because she jumped up and disappeared down the steps back to the pew. Andrew kept his gaze on the vicar.

The vicar was mumbling something, one hand held out towards Andrew, but he was some distance away. Why doesn't he come up and put a hand on my head, wondered Andrew, like he did for Elaine and Liz? But the vicar moved on quickly to the next kneeling child.

Goodness, thought Andrew, how white he looks. Christmas must be very hard work for vicars. Tiring. He gave the vicar an understanding smile. Then he rose to his feet, tucking Rupert inside his anorak as best he could, and swung round.

Down in the main church he could see the baby's mother standing up, jiggling the baby up and down. But nothing would still its roars, so she tiptoed out to the door, which clonked behind her. Anyone could have told her it was silly to bring a baby to church, thought Andrew. No idea how to behave. Now Rupert was another matter.

He walked back to the pew smiling so happily that his mum asked him what he was so pleased about.

She was no wiser when he answered.

"The blessing. It worked. God woke him up to hear it."

On the way out of church, Andrew was thinking about his three cousins who were coming to dinner, and his new football. All his cousins were boys, which was a good thing. There should be time for a proper game after dinner.

It took ages getting out of the church, there were so many people, all squashed against each other. At the door Andrew felt in his anorak to make sure Rupert was still all right. He wasn't there.

They had reached the car before Andrew could make his mother listen. "It's Rupert. He's gone."

"I expect he's on the pew seat," said his

father. "Don't worry, no one will take an old teddy."

Andrew was desperate. "No, you don't understand. He could crawl off, he could be stolen, he could be *killed*!"

Liz said nastily, "Serves you right for taking a snake to church."

"A *what*?" said his mum.

"A snake," said Liz.

His mum turned on him. "You brought the *snake*?"

Andrew said, "But you told us to bring our most special toys or animals."

"Oh Andrew. She meant toy animals, not real ones," said his father.

"Of course I thought you had the bear," said his mother. "We can't go back and look now, the turkey will burn and James and Kathleen and the three boys will be waiting outside our house."

His father said, "He can't have gone far. Better to look this afternoon, when the church is empty."

"I really cannot face the new vicar to tell him we've let a snake loose in his church," said his mum.

"What's *wrong* with a snake?" asked Andrew. "I keep telling everybody, he's not dangerous."

"That's not the point," snapped his mother, getting in behind the wheel, revving up the engine and pulling out into the road with unusual speed. She seemed pretty upset.

The turkey wasn't burnt, and Uncle James and Aunt Kathleen and the cousins had only been waiting five minutes when they reached home. Christmas dinner was terrific, or it would have been if only Rupert hadn't been missing, thought Andrew.

At last, when the last piece of Christmas pudding had been eaten by Uncle James, the last cracker pulled, the last cup of coffee drunk by the grown-ups, and Uncle James and Dad were stretched out in chairs on either side of the fire half asleep, Andrew followed his mother into the kitchen.

"Please? *Now* can we go and look for Rupert?"

Aunt Kathleen said, "I'll go. You've done enough. Come on Andrew, you can show me the way. I'll come with you."

The two of them hurried back to the church on foot. Luckily the door was not locked, and they slipped inside. The candles were no longer alight, and the church was much colder. Over in the far corner, the spotlight still shone down on the crib, on the Christ Child in the manger, on the wooden donkey and the shepherds, on Mary and Joseph and the three kings.

They started by trying to find the pew where Andrew had sat. Andrew wished now that his mum had come. He wasn't sure which one it had been.

Aunt Kathleen was very helpful, saying, "Well, never mind, we'll look under them all," but they couldn't find Rupert anywhere.

They looked where all the ivy and holly was twined around the pulpit, they looked in all the corners, they looked by the font, but he wasn't there. Andrew lay on his tummy and looked under the chest where the prayer books were kept, but he wasn't there.

They even went up the altar steps, and lifted up the cloth and looked under the altar, but he wasn't there either.

Aunt Kathleen said at last, "I don't think we're going to find him."

Stories for Six Year Olds

"But we've *got* to," said Andrew. "I *promised* to look after him."

Aunt Kathleen said, "One last look."

Andrew said, "D'you think God might help us find him?"

Aunt Kathleen said with a sigh, "I'm not sure that God—" but Andrew was already back across the church to the crib.

He screwed up his eyes and said, out loud, "Jesus, please let me find Rupert. After all," he added, "it was your fault for waking him up."

He opened his eyes and looked down, and there, in shadow, coiled up again and quite still on the flagstone floor, half hidden under one of the pews, was the snake. Fast asleep.

With a cry of joy Andrew gathered him up and put him in his anorak pocket, properly inside this time, and did up the zip.

"There, I told you we'd find him."

When they returned to Andrew's house the others were just starting tea. It was too dark for football now, but never mind, thought Andrew, it had been much more important to look for the snake.

"Did you find him?" asked Uncle James, his mouth full of Christmas cake. "Whatsisname. Rupert?"

"Yes," said Andrew, going upstairs to put him back in his box. "But he's not called Rupert now. He's called Noel, because he's a Christmas snake. Noel the First."

The Stinky Tree

David Henry Wilson

The Stinky Tree

David Henry Wilson

You've never heard of a stinky tree, have you? It's not surprising, because there's no such thing. But there *was* such a thing once, and you can think yourself lucky that you never went near it.

The stinky tree smelt like a combination of a gorilla's armpits after twelve rounds with the heavyweight champion, your feet after you've run twenty miles on a hot day, and a cow's bottom ten seconds after a stomach upset. Only it smelt even worse than that, if you can imagine *anything* smelling worse than that.

Now you might not have realised it, but trees are actually the kindest creatures in the world. They give away their fruit, they provide shelter for all kinds of birds, animals and insects, they supply us with wood and leaf mould, they help to balance air and water, and they look beautiful. If ever a creature deserved a medal for good nature, it's the tree.

But there's always someone somewhere who tries to spoil things, and the stinky tree was that someone.

"Why should I give my fruit away?" he cried. "I grew it, so it's mine. And why should all you birds, animals and insects twitter, munch and grub all over me? I'm private property, that's what I am, and I belong to me, not to you. So go away!"

He said this on a Monday morning. Nobody knew quite why he suddenly decided to become a nasty tree, but Mondays can do funny things to people, so maybe they do funny things to trees as well.

The Stinky Tree

Now before this fateful Monday morning, the stinky tree was not stinky at all. It was a perfectly normal tree, with blossoms in the spring, fruit in the summer, and no problems. The problems started when it told the birds, animals and insects to go away.

"But we live here!" they all whistled, squeaked or buzzed. "This is our home!"

"You lived here," said the tree, "and it was your home. Now you don't and it's not. Whistle, squeak and buzz off."

"Where will we go?"

"That's not my concern. My concern is me. Goodbye."

So the birds, animals and insects flew, ran and crawled off into the next field to hold a conference.

"What are we going to dowoowoowoo?" asked the owl.

"I shall just go nuts," squeaked the squirrel.

"And I shall go round the bend," said the caterpillar.

Of course there were plenty of trees in the neighbourhood, but they all seemed pretty full, and a quick call to the Ministry of Nesting revealed that there was in fact a shortage of accommodation in the area.

"There are no empty trees ariaound," said the official (who was a bureaucat). "You'll have to nest on the griaound."

But everyone knew that ground nesting was far too dangerous. The bureaucat knew it as well, which might be why he suggested it.

Fortunately the trees themselves were much more sympathetic, and before long, offers were coming in:

"I'll take one," said a plum.

"Give me two," said a yew.

The Stinky Tree

"And I can take three," said a horse-chestnut tree.

"Then I'll manage four," cried a tall sycamore.

"Let's have five," said a chive.

"Hold it!" cried the other trees. "You're a herb, not a tree!"

"I know," said the chive, "but I rhyme with five."

And so it went on, right up to a date which took eight, a pine which took nine, and finally the world-record-breaker, a bamboo which took twenty-two.

At last, every one of the birds, animals and insects had found a new home, and the forest was able to settle down again. But no-one was happy about the nasty tree's behaviour. Such selfishness, they felt, should not be ignored, and so another conference was held in order to work out a suitable punishment.

How would *you* have punished the selfish tree? Perhaps you'd have taken away its fruit, stripped off its leaves, smacked its bottom, or sent it to bed without any supper. But the birds, animals and insects worked out an even better punishment, which all of them could help to impose.

You see, all birds, animals and insects have to eat and drink, just like us. And just like us, they have to get rid of the waste that they can't digest. They tend to let it out wherever they happen to be at the time, which is why you can be walking innocently along the road and suddenly find something soft and smelly sticking to your foot or – even worse – landing on your head.

The punishment to be given to the selfish tree was that in future all the waste matter would be left on it, over it, or under it. The selfish tree was to become the forest toilet.

Before long, the selfish tree had become the stinky tree, and every leaf, twig, branch and root was covered in dung. The birds took to dropping their waste matter from ever greater heights, while the animals and insects simply held their breath while they performed, and then scurried away as fast as their legs or wings could carry them.

As for the stinky tree itself, it would also have scurried away if it had had legs or wings to scurry with. But not only are trees unable to move, they're also unable to defend themselves, and so the coating of brown and

The Stinky Tree

white became ever thicker, and the smell became ever stinkier.

"Please... phew... please... ouf!" cried the selfish tree. "No more... ugh... no more... yuck! I'm sorry for what I did, and I'll never be selfish again!"

It even promised to take all the birds and animals and insects back again, but of course none of them wanted to nest in a tree that smelt worse than a gorilla's armpit, a sweaty foot, and a cow's bottom all rolled into one.

There was one big problem with this punishment, and it was a problem that soon required an urgent solution. The smell from the stinky tree didn't confine itself to the stinky tree alone. It spread. And the longer the punishment went on, the wider the effect was felt. Eventually, the whole forest was holding its nose and longing for the good old days of stinklessness.

And although the stinky tree had apologized, all the birds, animals and insects had got into the habit of leaving their dung there, and habits are very difficult things to change. So the smell got worse, and worse, and worse...

Stories for Six Year Olds

The Stinky Tree

How was it made to go away? And why are there no stinky trees now? Well, it's all thanks to two insects, one of which was a fly, and one of which was a beetle. People often ask what use are flies and beetles, and the answer is that some flies and some beetles are simply brilliant when it comes to stink-removal. Do you know how they do it? If you want to know, read on.

The flies and the beetles lay their eggs in dung. Yes, they do. That may seem a funny place to lay eggs, but since you've never laid an egg yourself, how do you know which is a funny place and which is a normal place? Maybe the flies and the beetles reckon that nobody would fancy eating eggs laid in dung, and so their babies will be quite safe there. Would you like an egg covered in dung? Of course you wouldn't, so the flies and the beetles aren't stupid, are they?

When the eggs hatch into larvae, they eat the dung. Now *you* wouldn't want to eat dung, would you? But again that shows how clever the flies and beetles are, because they know that nobody else is going to take their food from them. So they can eat away to their hearts' content.

And that's how the problem of the stinky tree was solved. The flies and beetles went out and laid their eggs in the muck, then their larvae popped out of the eggs, and gobbled it all up. Each larva grew nice and fat, the muck soon disappeared, the smell disappeared with it, the birds, animals and insects made their nests in the tree again, and the tree was very happy to have them back.

It was some time before all the other birds, animals and insects got used to leaving their dung elsewhere in the forest, but the flies and beetles just went on laying their eggs there till the habit was broken. And now if you mention the stinky tree, nobody will know which tree you mean. The only trace that remains is the name given to the tree when the flies and beetles moved in, for even today we still talk of going to the larvatree.

My Brother is a Pig

Sharon Creech

My Brother is a Pig

Sharon Creech

I didn't mean to turn my brother into a pig, but I did, and it happened like this:

On Saturdays, my dad likes to clomp around car boot sales searching for treasures, and I like to go with him. My little brother Joey usually tags along too, but he is always a royal pain, whingeing on about how tired he is and how hungry and how hot or how cold.

You'd be amazed at what people practically

give away at these sales. They stuff their car boots with all sorts of things which they are more than happy to sell to complete strangers.

We always come home with something. This doesn't make my mother too pleased, because she thinks it is all junk, but she just doesn't use her imagination.

It was at one of these sales that I found the magic kit. It was tucked under a pile of old games and puzzles in a car boot. A gnarly old lady with a pointy nose and no teeth was bent over her treasures, taping little bitty price tags to things. Every now and then she'd stop and squeeze her hands together and roll them around each other as if she were rolling an invisible snowball.

I noticed the word MAGIC on the corner of a box and asked the gnarly old lady if I could look at it. She rolled her hands around and licked her lips. "Sure, my little one, sure you can." Her voice sounded as if it came out of the back of her nose.

Joey was tugging at my shirt. "I'm hungry, Claire, I'm *hungry*!"

"Let go," I said. "Let me just look at this magic kit, will you?"

"I'm *hungry*, Claire. I'm *cold*."

The magic kit box was dented and one corner chewed off, but the things inside looked as if they had never been used. There were two silk scarves, three plastic cups, a crystal, a rolled up tube of papery flowers, a magic wand, a booklet of magic spells, and three tiny bottles containing coloured liquids.

I bought it. As I walked away, the gnarly old woman said, "Heh, heh, heh. You be careful there. You be real careful."

"I'm *hungry*, Claire," Joey wailed. "I'm cold. I'm tired."

On the way home, Joey kept trying to grab my magic set.

"Get away," I said. "It's mine."

"Daaaaad," Joey wailed. "Dad, Claire won't let me look at the magic thingy."

"Let him see it," my dad said.

Joey dumped all the contents of the box onto the seat and got his sticky fingers all over everything. "I want this," he said, holding up one of the silk scarves and putting it on his head.

"Let go," I said. "It's mine. Put it back."

"Daaaad—"

It was like that all the way home. I tried to ignore him. I was leafing through the booklet of spells, but I couldn't concentrate with him dropping things on the floor and messing everything up. I noticed a couple of strange words in the book: *palulah* and *padiddle* and *padong*. *Padong* seemed pretty important because it was used a lot, and there was even a picture of a magician holding up the magic wand and saying, "*Padong!*" All sorts of fireworks were exploding out of his magic wand. It looked really good.

Crack! Joey had sat on one of the plastic cups.

"Look at what you've done," I said. "You nincompoop."

"Daaaad—" Joey cried.

Woosh! The yellow silk scarf on Joey's head blew out of the window.

"Hey – that's mine – it's gone – you triple nincompoop—"

"Daaaad—"

When we got home, I snatched the remains of my magic kit and ran upstairs. I was examining the magic wand when Joey came to the door.

"I want to do magic," he said. "I want to. *Now*."

"You'd better watch it," I warned. "Or I'll turn you into something dreadful."

"You will not."

"I will. I'll turn you into a-a-a pig! A slobbery, ugly, fat pig!"

"You will not."

"I will too." I waved the wand in the air. "*Palulah! Padiddle!*" I waved the wand around his head. "*Padong!*"

Fireworks spurted out of the wand and blue smoke filled the air and there was a tremendous popping and crunching sound and then – *Snort! Snort!*

I dropped the magic wand.

There at my feet was a big, hairy, fat, slobbery pig. It looked up at me with a puzzled expression. *Snort! Snort!*

My brother was a pig.

Snort! Snort! My pig brother shoved his fat snout at my legs. His pink and grey hooves trampled my feet. He started rooting around the room, pushing his snout into my clothes and my duvet, slobbering over everything in sight.

Stories for Six Year Olds

My Brother is a Pig

"Quit it," I said. "Turn back into Joey. Go away, pig."

The pig scrabbled under my bed and out the other side. It trotted all around the room, pushing and slobbering and making a terrible mess.

I picked up the wand. *"Padiddle-ulah." "Padoddle-paliddle."* I couldn't remember the words. Where was that booklet? I searched my desk, my bed, the floor.

The pig charged at me. It was carrying something in its mouth.

"Drop it," I said, pulling the torn, wet, slobber-covered booklet from the pig's mouth.

"Palulah! Padiddle!" I read as I waved the wand around the pig's head. *"Padong!"*

Fireworks burst into the air. Blue smoke swirled all around.

Snort! Snort! Snort! Snort!

Now there were *two* pigs. They chased each other around the room, knocking over my chair and my lamp. They pulled the duvet onto the floor and dragged it under the bed.

I dashed for the door and leaped into the hall, closing the door quickly behind me.

I had a feeling I was in deep, deep trouble.

I crept downstairs. "Dad?"

"Where's Joey?" he said. "Are you watching him?"

"He's upstairs."

"What's all that racket? It sounds like a herd of animals. Go and see what he's up to."

"Joey's a pig, Dad."

"Don't call your brother a pig."

"No, I mean he *really* is a pig. Two pigs, actually."

"Claire, that's enough of that. Don't talk that way about your brother."

"Will you *listen* to me?" I said. "He's big and fat and slobbery and—"

"Claire, you stop that this instant. Up to your room. *Now*! Not another word out of you."

Reluctantly, I crept back upstairs. There was a terrible snorting and crashing coming from my room. I peeked inside.

The room was a shambles: furniture toppled this way and that, the lamp broken, clothes strewn across the floor, papers chewed. The pigs were in the midst of chomping their way through my science book.

Maybe I should feed them. Maybe it would calm them down.

My Brother is a Pig

In the kitchen I grabbed the biggest bowl I could find. In it I dumped a box of cereal and a bottle of milk. It looked like the sort of slop a pig might eat. But it was not quite disgusting enough. What else did pigs eat? Maybe they ate worms.

Outside, I dug around the fence until I found three slimy worms. I chopped them up and added them to the cereal.

As I was sneaking back upstairs, my father appeared.

"Claire! Didn't I send you to your room?"

"I'm just going."

"What in the world have you got in that bowl?"

"Food," I said.

"Well, don't make a pig of yourself."

"I'll try very hard not to."

"And make Joey stop that racket up there."

"I'll try very hard," I said.

Upstairs, the pigs had finished my science book and were rooting around for something else. "Here piggies," I said. "Come and get some slop."

They buried their heads in the bowl, pushing and shoving and slurping. Cereal-worm-mash splattered everywhere. They cleaned out that bowl in five seconds flat and then they crawled under my bed, dragging the duvet with them, and fell asleep.

I grabbed the magic booklet and frantically leafed through it. Bits were missing.

There was a knock on the door, followed by Dad's head peering around it. "*What* in the world—?" He looked at the toppled furniture, the broken lamp, the trampled clothes. "This place looks like a pig sty!"

"Exactly," I agreed.
"Claire, get this cleaned up right now!"

My Brother is a Pig

"I think you should look under my bed," I said. I figured I'd better get it over with. He'd better see for himself.

"No thank you," he said coldly. "I've seen quite enough. You have exactly one hour to clean up this pig sty before your mother gets home." He slammed the door.

I didn't know what to do. I sat down on my bed. "I wish it was like it used to be," I said, skimming through the booklet. Then I saw these words: *"How to reverse a spell."*

Hurray! That was it. I read the directions. It said to dip the magic wand in each of the three bottles of coloured liquids: first into the red one, then the blue one, then the yellow one. Then, while the wand was still wet, wave it over the object and say the first two words in reverse order: first *padiddle*, then *palulah*. Wave the wand again and shout *Padong*! twice.

I found the three bottles of liquid, put them on my desk, opened them and dipped the wand in the red one, then the blue one, and lastly in the yellow one. I jumped on my bed. *"Padiddle! Palulah!"* I waved the wand again. *"Padong! Padong!"*

Tremendous fireworks spurted all around. The bottles of liquid toppled off the desk, spilling onto the carpet. Blue smoke whizzed around the room. I fell to the floor.

"Daaaad—"

And there in front of me was Joey, sitting on my duvet, his mouth covered with the cereal-worm slop. "Daaaad—" he wailed.

I was never so happy to see a slop-covered brother in all my life. I tried to hug him, but he ran out of the room. "Daaaad—" he cried.

You can imagine how relieved I was.

Now I have only one problem. Somehow, in reversing that last magic spell, I not only turned two pigs back into one Joey, but I turned my bed into a tree.

That's going to take some explaining.

Another Hodder Children's book

Best Stories For Under Fives

Help a rabbit find his way to Australia, find out why Huffalo Buffalo thinks the sky is about to fall in and watch out for a baby crocodile with terrible toothache.

An irresistible collection of stories specially written by Sam McBratney, Julia Jarman, Vivian French, Carolyn Hart, Anthony Lishak, Tony Kenyon, Francesca Simon and Jenny Koralek *just* for under fives.

Another Hodder Children's book

Best Stories For Five Year Olds

Meet a little girl who turns into a mouse, find out the trouble with having an anteater for a pet and dance with a magical palm tree!

An exceptional collection of stories specially written by Joan Aiken, Joyce Dunbar, Ann Turnbull, Karen Wallace, Geoffrey Patterson, David Sutherland, Jenny Alexander and Kathy Henderson *just* for five year olds.

Another Hodder Children's book

Best Stories For Seven Year Olds

Watch out for a bear in the bathroom, talk to some magical pigeons, and find out what cows are doing in the classroom!

A lively collection of stories specially written by Vivien Alcock, Joan Aiken, Elizabeth Laird, Stephen Elboz and Sharon Creech *just* for seven year olds.

Another Hodder Children's book

Five Minutes To Bed

Read about the secret of Josh's magical stones, and discover what lives under the stairs...

Meet the girl who frog-hops to the moon, and a sad see-through pig who just wants to be pink!

A delightful collection of bedtime stories by Joan Aiken, Margaret Mahy, Joyce Dunbar and Karen Wallace to name but a few, all selected by children's book reviewer, Julia Eccleshare.

HODDER STORY COLLECTIONS

0340 646322	BEST STORIES FOR UNDER FIVES	£2.99	❏
0340 646330	BEST STORIES FOR FIVE YEAR OLDS	£2.99	❏
0340 646349	BEST STORIES FOR SIX YEAR OLDS	£2.99	❏
0340 646357	BEST STORIES FOR SEVEN YEAR OLDS	£2.99	❏
0340 626577	FIVE MINUTES TO BED	£3.50	❏

BOOK AND TAPE PACKS

185998 3146	BEST STORIES FOR UNDER FIVES	£5.99	❏
185998 3154	BEST STORIES FOR FIVE YEAR OLDS	£5.99	❏
185998 3162	BEST STORIES FOR SIX YEAR OLDS	£5.99	❏
185998 3170	BEST STORIES FOR SEVEN YEAR OLDS	£5.99	❏
185998 4126	FIVE MINUTES TO BED	£5.99	❏

All Hodder Children's books are available at your local bookshop or newsagent, or can be ordered direct from the publisher. Just tick the titles you want and fill in the form below. Prices and availability subject to change without notice.

Hodder Children's Books, Cash Sales Department, Bookpoint, 39 Milton Park, Abingdon, OXON, OX14 4TD, UK. If you have a credit card you may order by telephone – 0235 831700.

Please enclose a cheque or postal order made payable to Bookpoint Ltd to the value of the cover price and allow the following for postage and packing:
UK & BFPO – £1.00 for the first book, 50p for the second book, and 30p for each additional book ordered up to a maximum charge of £3.00.
OVERSEAS & EIRE – £2.00 for the first book, £1.00 for the second book, and 50p for each additional book.

Name..

Address...

....

....
If you would prefer to pay by credit card, please complete:
Please debit my Visa/Access/Diner's Card/American Express (delete as applicable) card no:

Signature..

Expiry Date..